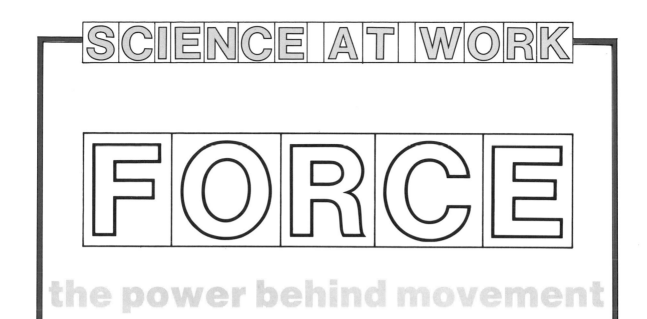

SCIENCE AT WORK

FORCE

the power behind movement

Eric Laithwaite

Franklin Watts
London New York Toronto Sydney

© 1986 Franklin Watts

First published in 1986 by
Franklin Watts
12a Golden Square
London W1

First published in the USA by
Franklin Watts Inc.
387 Park Avenue South
New York, N.Y. 10016

First published in Australia by
Franklin Watts Australia
14 Mars Road
Lane Cove
NSW 2066

UK ISBN: 0 86313 341 X
US ISBN: 0-531-10181-9
Library of Congress
Catalog Card No:
85-52047

Printed in Belgium

Designed by Ben White

Illustrated by Hayward Art
    Group

Photographs:
British Aerospace   18
Cementation Piling and
    Foundation   10
Chris Fairclough   4, 11, 13,
    15, 16, 17, 19, 20, 23, 26,
    28
Lewmar Marine (photo by
    Willoughby Stewart
    Associates Ltd)   25
NASA   5
ZEFA   6, 7, 9

Contents

Gravity

Force is something we *feel*. We are conscious of being pulled downward, toward the Earth, from the day we are born (and even before we are conscious of it). We call this the force of gravity. There are other kinds of force, too, and we shall look at each in turn.

Very small babies love dropping objects over the edges of their high chairs. They don't know it, but they are seeing examples of gravity at work. For most of us this is the beginning of science, for like gravity many other things always behave in the same way for the same conditions. If it were not so, our very existence would be insecure.

Force is something we can measure — so are *length* and *time*. On these three the whole of mechanical science is built.

▷ Although the parachutist seems to float down slowly, he lands with the same sort of bump as when jumping off a small stepladder.

◁ See the delight on the child's face as the result of *knowing* exactly what will happen when she drops the object.

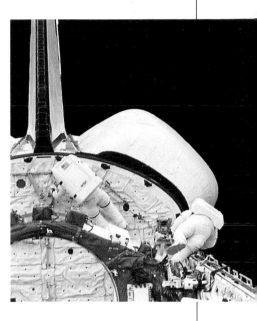

▷ Astronauts in zero gravity have no sensation of "falling," because they do not change speed. Nor can they "float," for they experience no force at all.

Without gravity, all loose objects would float away from the Earth. In outer space, a long way from Earth, there is very little gravity, and all objects appear to float freely. Astronauts in outer space are aware that there is no longer a feeling of "up" or "down." Things do not have a "top" and a "bottom." Such ideas only belong in places where the force of gravity is present.

A parachutist feels no force of gravity within his body when he first jumps from the plane because he falls freely. But once his parachute opens, he feels gravity again. The straps that fasten him to the 'chute are pulling up on his frame while his inside is being pulled down by gravity. He floats down slowly in this condition. What is happening to the parachute is that its large area receives an upward force from the air that is rushing into it. This upward force *opposes* the force on the straps due to gravity acting on the heavy body of the parachutist.

5

Using gravity

We use the force of gravity in all kinds of ways. Gravity gives us our sense of what is *vertical* — at right angles to the surface of the Earth. So when we hang a weight on the end of a string or rope, we know that the string hangs vertically. This is used to help us build our houses with vertical walls that will not topple over.

A skier uses the force of gravity to get a free ride down the slope. As long as a body is moving nearer to the center of the Earth, even though not directly toward it, gravity will provide the force to push it along.

If water is channeled so that it falls on the blades of a paddle wheel, the water will turn the wheel, which can be used to do work, such as generating electric power. A river can be made to do this.

Water in a river flows downhill for the same reason that the skier gets a free ride — it is moving nearer to the center of the Earth.

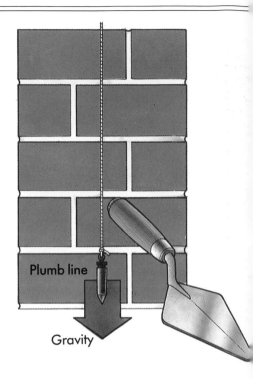

△ A bricklayer's plumb line makes use of gravity to find the vertical.

◁ A skier on a slope could be said to be "falling" under the force of gravity, except that the force has been reduced in size by the angle of the slope.

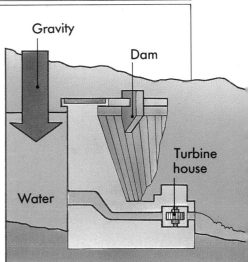

△ The wall or dam is built high to allow the water to build up to a great height behind it. In this way it will apply a huge force to the blades of the turbine as it falls on them from the top of the dam. The electric generators are connected directly to the turbines in the turbine house.

If instead all the water flowing in a river merely runs into the sea, all the valuable energy will be wasted. But if we build a wall or dam across the river, we can control the flow of water and make it turn a specially designed paddle wheel called a turbine, which then drives large electric generators.

We use the effect of gravity on water when we design a water supply for a house or for a whole town or city. The water must be stored in a reservoir *higher* than any of the houses it is to supply so that it can run *down* the pipes to feed the houses. A sewage system operates in the same way, except that the houses must now be *higher* than the tank or other receptacle for the sewage.

Engineering is the art of using the natural forces and materials of the universe, such as the force of gravity, to make our lives better. An engineer tries to invent new devices, new processes and new ways of thinking about things, always with a view to doing them more profitably.

Inertia

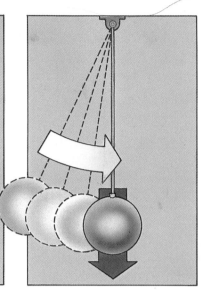

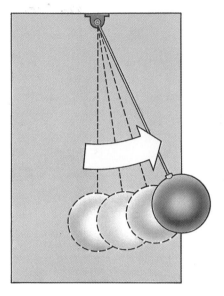

It takes a force to start an object moving, or to stop it when it is moving. We say this is because the object has "inertia." In the same way it takes a force to make an object move faster or to make it slow down. It also takes a force to make a moving object change its direction of movement.

A pendulum only continues to swing past its lowest point because of inertia. When the bob is pulled aside and released, it begins to swing down to the lowest point for the same reason that a skier rushes downhill. The force of gravity, reduced in both these cases because the movement is at an angle to the vertical, is trying to pull the mass nearer to the center of the Earth.

But once the pendulum has reached the lowest possible point, like the plumb-line, the only reason that it swings on *beyond* this point is that it is now moving and its inertia requires a *force* to slow it down. This force can only be supplied by gravity once it has passed the lowest point and started to climb away from the Earth again.

△ **1** When the line is pulled aside, the initial force is provided by gravity, acting, as it were, down a "slope."
2 At the lowest point gravity acts vertically downward.
3 Inertia provides the means for the pendulum to climb up again on the other side of the lowest position.

Every object must have inertia, for without it any force, however small when applied to the object, would immediately propel it at infinite speed!

We use inertia forces when we use a hammer to knock in nails or to break pieces of hard rock. The hardness of the rock means that the hammer must be stopped in a very short distance. The hammer's inertia therefore produces a very large force. This force splits the rock.

On a much larger scale, inertia forces are used to knock down old buildings. A very heavy metal ball on the end of a chain is accelerated by swinging it from a crane and aiming it at the side of the building. By moving the crane rapidly sideways the ball is first lifted against gravity so as to become a pendulum. The process generally has to be repeated many times before the demolition is complete.

▽ Once the wall is broken, moving pieces of brick themselves knock out further bricks by their own inertia. Often the initial force of the ball will take it right through a solid wall.

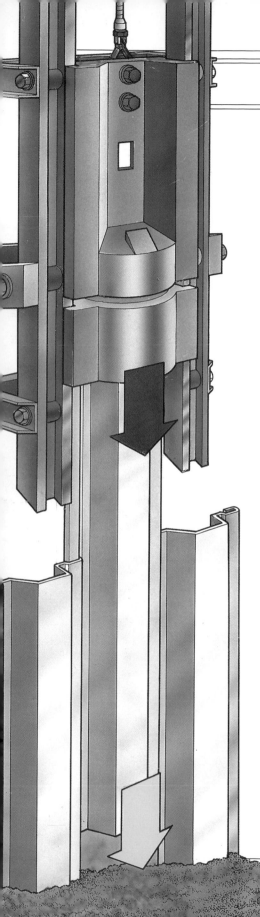

Working together

It is not often that we see the forces of gravity and inertia working independently. Generally they are both involved in any one action, as in the case of a pile driver.

A heavy weight is wound up by hand or by a motor and then released so that it falls under the force of gravity. It accelerates all the time it is falling. By the time it hits the pile, it is moving rapidly. The impact with the stationary pile delivers an enormous inertial force to the pile, driving it into the ground.

A more everyday example is a hammer used for driving in nails. If you simply lift the hammer and let it fall, gravity does most of the work for you. The bigger the hammer head, the bigger the force will be.

A pile driver is really a long hammer with no handle. It is guided on to the target in grooves. Like a hammer, it is used for driving things in.

But a large blow can also be delivered if you force the hammer down as it is moving, making it drop faster than it would under gravity alone. It seems easier to press down on the handle as it is moving than to lift a heavy hammer against gravity. It is therefore possible to use quite a small hammer to deliver a large blow.

It is interesting to see the different shapes of hammer used for different jobs. Where the head is chubby — almost a sphere — it will deliver a short, sharp blow suitable for chipping stone. This is the stonemason's hammer. A long cylindrical hammer head will deliver a longer, sustained force. This is the type needed for pile drivers or for driving nails into wood, where the material is more yielding to the force and moves along with the hammer for some distance.

△ The handle of a hammer is used to increase the speed. The stronger the user, the longer the handle will generally be. Compare the handle lengths of the road builder's hammer and the common household hammer.

Friction

▽ When a file is used on a piece of metal, the sharp ridges of the file actually cut pieces of metal from the material. These are known as "filings." Finer files and sandpaper actually do the same thing but on a much smaller scale.

Friction

Another important natural force is the force of friction. Without it we could not grip objects in order to pick them up, we could not walk along, we could not fasten things together, and the whole world would be forever filled with sliding objects!

All things which touch each other have a frictional force between them when you try to slide them over each other. This is because their surfaces are rough and they tend to "lock" together. Even surfaces that seem smooth to the naked eye are found to be as uneven as a plowed field when viewed through a microscope. Frictional forces are the result of roughness all the way down to microscopic level.

Even moving liquids have frictional forces within the liquid itself, which tend always to slow down the movement. We call these forces viscosity. A gas is simply a "thinner" kind of liquid in which the viscous forces are smaller, but still large enough to

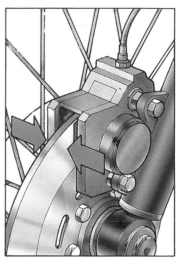

have considerable effects. Liquids and gases can be conveniently classed together as "fluids."

Sometimes we want to make frictional forces as small as possible, but more often we make use of friction, often unconsciously.

When we use a file, we want as much friction as possible, so the file is made with very rough surfaces. In the same way, when we want to slow down vehicles with wheels, we put very rough discs on the shafts and on the fixed parts of the vehicle. When we apply the brakes, we make these two rough surfaces come in contact with each other over a large area.

Whenever sliding takes place against friction, heat is produced between the surfaces in contact. We have to be sure that the heat is not so great that the materials that are rubbing together catch fire, or are otherwise damaged by the heat.

When we make machines, friction is generally seen as a nuisance. It lowers efficiency and generates unwanted heat. Yet without friction, the machine itself would fall to pieces!

△ If the brakes of a car or motorbike are applied for too long a period (when going down a long, steep hill, for example) the heat may burn out the surfaces of the brake pads, which then become dangerously ineffective. This is why motorists are advised to use low gear when descending steep hills.

Reducing friction

Friction forces in fluids are a great deal less than most of the friction forces between solid objects. If therefore we wish to make things slide easily over each other, one way is to introduce some liquid between the two.

Liquids used in this way are called "lubricants," and the whole subject of making moving parts slide easily over each other is known as lubrication.

Water can be quite an effective lubricant for surfaces that are not affected by it chemically, for example where it does not produce rusting, as it would on iron. You can try this with two glass plates or mirrors. Although the surfaces appear very smooth and flat, you probably won't be able to make them slide over each other unless water is introduced between them. Then the forces opposing sliding become very small indeed.

▽ Often, two glass sheets appear to "stick" because of dirt particles that lie between them. Cleaning the glass helps a little, but water lubrication is much more effective, especially if the surfaces are cleaned before the water is added.

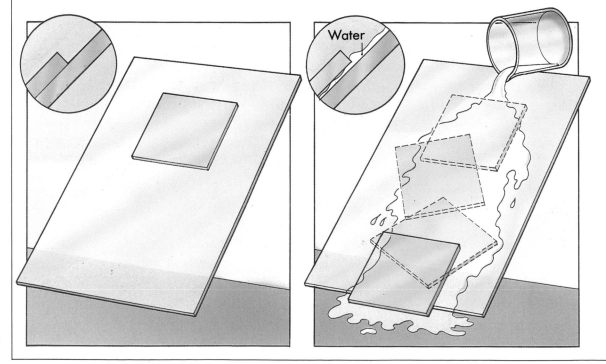

Water

▷ The cylinders in a car engine are usually water-cooled because a lot of heat is generated in them by the exploding fuel. The circulating oil tends to evaporate a little and some is lost through leaks, so new oil has to be added occasionally.

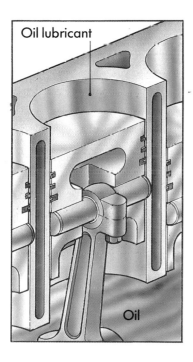

Oil lubricant

Oil

△ Friction forces are kept as low as possible by keeping the contact area between piston and cylinder as small as possible. This is done by using a few thin spring rings which fit into grooves in the piston. Only the rings make contact with the cylinder wall.

Oil is a very common liquid to use as a lubricant because unlike water it does not react chemically with metals. It doesn't evaporate easily either, so it does not have to be replaced frequently.

In machines like car engines, the most important part of the whole action is where pistons slide inside cylinders. When a car travels a thousand miles, each piston slides up and down its cylinder over a million times. If the piston is not to act like a file and wear away itself and the cylinder, the lubrication must be good enough to reduce the friction to a very low level indeed. This is achieved by pumping oil continuously into the cylinder to make sure that all surfaces are constantly lubricated. The same oil is used again and again in a circulating system.

In very special machines where the forces of friction have to be reduced below those possible with liquid lubrication, gas lubrication is used. The surfaces are separated by gas under pressure. Bearings of this kind are in fact known as "gas bearings."

15

Wheels

Friction caused by sliding one object over another depends upon the area of the surfaces in contact – the bigger the area, the greater the force. The frictional force from any area also depends on the forces pressing the surfaces together.

But if just one of the surfaces is curved so that it can *roll* over the other, in theory there is no sliding at all and therefore there should be no friction. Continuous rolling gives us the wheel.

Now wheels are never perfectly round, for the pressure on their rims deforms them slightly. You can see this easily on car tires, which have a small flattened area at the bottom where they are in contact with the road. The expansions and contractions that are necessary as each point in turn becomes flattened cause some friction.

This is known as rolling friction and it is considerably less than sliding friction. This is why wheels are so very useful.

▷ Steel wheels on steel rails have even less rolling friction than rubber tires because the flattening is much less. Rolling friction can be as low as possible for railroad cars, but the engines *need* friction to drive, like the car. This is obtained through the extra pressure provided by a heavy engine.

If you put a paint mark on a bicycle tire and ride the bike in a straight line so that some of the paint is transferred to the road, you can measure the distance between any successive pair of marks. Then measure the circumference of the tire using a tape measure with the bike lying on its side. You will find that it's greater than the distance between the road marks. The small difference is the amount the tire slipped on the road over that distance. This is the amount by which *rolling* friction is smaller than sliding friction, i.e. the friction you would need to overcome to push the bike the whole distance with the brakes on.

Rubber tires are not intended to reduce friction to zero, for the vehicle needs to push from the road in order to propel itself. Powerful cars are capable of spinning their wheels on the road if the over-eager driver does not mind wearing out the tires rapidly!

△ The grooves in rubber tires are designed to act as water pumps to force rainwater out sideways. Water under the wheel would act as a lubricant and cause the car to skid.

▷ Bearings at the centers of wheels should have as little friction as possible. Often a bearing is made of a ring of balls which roll around in a groove between the fixed and moving parts of the machine. Friction is then further reduced by using oil or grease. Have a look at the ball bearing on the back wheel of a bike.

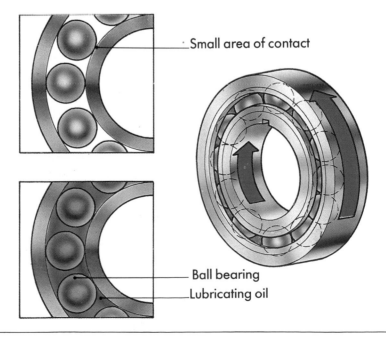

Small area of contact

Ball bearing

Lubricating oil

Combining forces

Very often the forces of gravity, inertia and friction all work together. For example, when a jet comes in to land, it relies on gravity to put pressure between wheels and runway. Friction can then slow the aircraft against its own inertia, which tries to keep it going forward. If the landing wheels are not spinning as they first hit the ground, they need an enormous acceleration before they are rolling at the right speed. This acceleration requires an inertia force which also slows the aircraft but produces a lot of skidding and tire wear. This can be seen from the smoke produced by the heat generated immediately on contact.

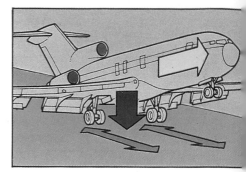

▽ An aircraft with 6-ft wheels landing at 200 mph needs the wheels to spin at about 900 revolutions per minute to avoid skidding.

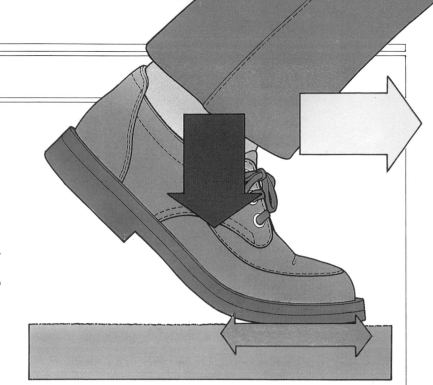

▷ When we walk, we use gravity to help provide our forward-going force. We use our muscles to make ourselves lean slightly forward so that our center of gravity is in front of the foot which is on the ground. Gravity pulls us both downward and forward, so that we have to put the other foot forward to avoid falling on our faces!

Even such a common action as walking uses quite a complicated combination of forces. We require a forward force to overcome our inertia and allow us to accelerate forward. We rely entirely on friction forces between the ground and our shoes to provide this force. In turn we rely on our weight, i.e. the force of gravity, to put enough pressure on the ground to give a big enough frictional force.

On slippery surfaces we need shoes with special soles to increase the friction. In extreme cases where high acceleration is necessary, for example on a running track, spiked running shoes are used which allow the athlete's foot to be temporarily nailed to the ground! When we lean forward, we imitate the skier on a slope. Watch how a sprinter leans forward at a much greater angle than someone walking.

In certain machining processes where we try to wear away a surface by friction, the weight of the grinder uses gravity and the operator opposes inertia manually.

△ The frictional force produced by a grinder is so intense that the heat makes the metal glow red hot. Most of this hot metal comes off as sparks.

Smooth forces

The forces that drive wheels are very often those made by pistons in cylinders. These forces are always jerky, whereas what the wheel usually needs is a steady turning force.

One way of smoothing out jerky forces is to use a flywheel. A flywheel is simply a wheel with a very large inertia.

The piston delivers a force to turn the wheel for only a small part of each revolution, and even then the force varies from instant to instant. A large flywheel is not accelerated very much by each stroke of the piston. But the combined effect of hundreds of such strokes eventually spins the wheel at very nearly constant speed.

The wheels of a bicycle act partly like flywheels, smoothing out each pedal push. Maximum force is always produced by the foot driving the pedal downward. Like the piston in the cylinder, it's a jerky motion rather than a steady driving force.

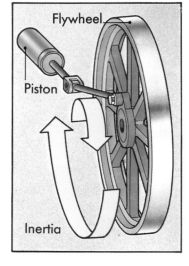

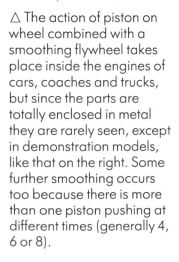

△ The action of piston on wheel combined with a smoothing flywheel takes place inside the engines of cars, coaches and trucks, but since the parts are totally enclosed in metal they are rarely seen, except in demonstration models, like that on the right. Some further smoothing occurs too because there is more than one piston pushing at different times (generally 4, 6 or 8).

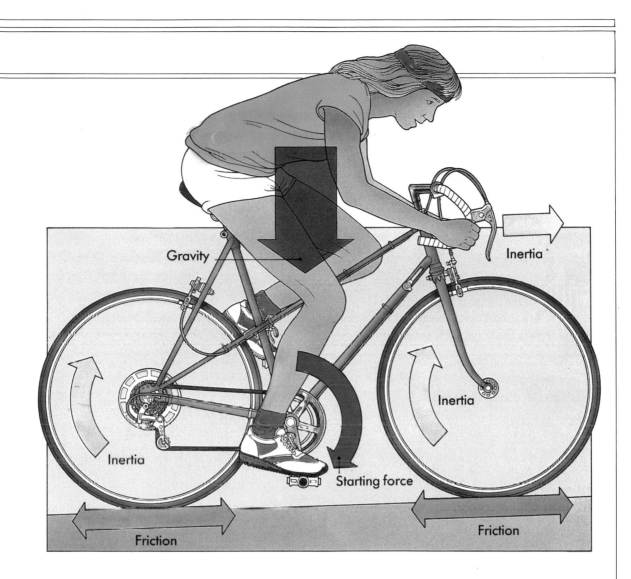

Gravity

Inertia

Inertia

Starting force

Inertia

Friction

Friction

Gravity
Without gravity there could be no propulsion, for the wheels would not be held down to the ground.

Friction
We *rely* on friction to push us along. Yet we must *reduce* friction in the bearings of all wheels.

Inertia
We overcome inertia to start. Once moving, the inertia of wheels, bike and rider gives us a smooth ride.

The inertia of the whole bicycle plus rider also helps to smooth out the force from the feet.

The driving force for bike and rider comes from the frictional force between the tires and the ground. At fast speeds, the biggest frictional force comes from the viscosity of the air through which rider and bike must pass.

Parallel forces

When two parallel forces act on an object in opposite directions, they produce a twisting effect and can cause objects to rotate.

Twisting forces are as common as forces in straight lines. Think how many you use every day at home — turning on faucets, turning door handles, using a screwdriver, screwing lids on jars and medicine bottles. Twisting forces are things we tend to take for granted.

In engineering, all machines with wheels, gears and pulleys need twisting forces to drive them. They themselves pass on twisting forces along shafts. A car uses mostly twisting forces in its internal workings, yet its purpose is to produce motion in more or less a straight line.

▷ A screwdriver makes use of parallel forces as each side of the blade pushes in opposite directions on the ends of the slot wall in the screw. The type of screwdriver and screw shown are only one of several types in use today. In some there are 4 blades on the screwdriver and a pair of crossed slots at 90° to each other in the screwhead. Here 2 pairs of parallel forces could be said to act on the screw, but there could have been only 3 blades and 3 slots — so twisting forces need not necessarily go in pairs.

Parallel forces

22

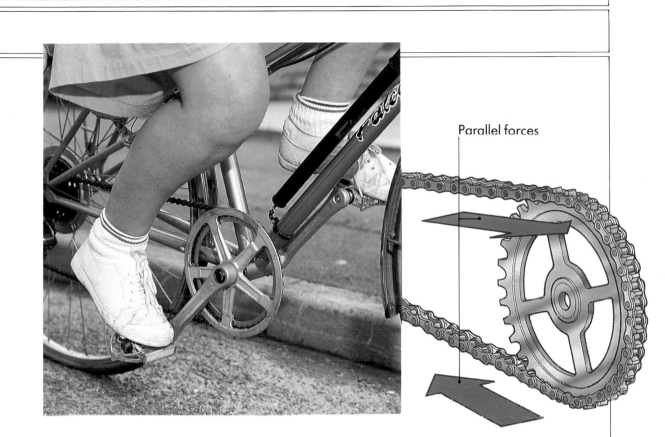

Parallel forces

The best place to see the conversion from twisting to straight line forces is in a bicycle chain.

When a cyclist pushes the pedals, the forces turn the chain wheel. But the twisting forces on the chain wheel are immediately turned back into two straight line forces along the top and bottom parts of the chain.

At the back wheel axle a second chain wheel converts the two forces back into a twisting force that turns the back wheel. The final conversion is made by the back wheel itself, using the force of friction between tire and ground. The forward force propels the bicycle and rider; the reverse force at the ground pushes the Earth backward!

It is, of course, just the same when you walk. Every step forward pushes the Earth backward, but by only a microscopic distance because of the relative sizes of the Earth and the walker.

▽ To turn on a faucet a pair of parallel forces may be applied using finger and thumb only. Or the whole top may be grasped in the hand, when it is difficult to say where the single forces are acting.

23

Levers and gears

Extra large twisting forces can be applied by using a lever. Every time you use a wrench to fasten or unfasten a nut you are using a lever. The amount of twisting force you apply to the nut is related to the length of the handle of the wrench. If the handle is only half as long, you will need to push twice as hard to undo the nut.

You can see levers being used in all kinds of everyday situations. When you lift the handles of a wheelbarrow, you do not have to apply as much force as the weight in the wheelbarrow, simply because that weight is so much nearer the wheel. A well-designed wheelbarrow will have its load right over the wheel. Then it only has to be pushed — no lifting force at all is necessary.

▽ Such enormous force can be obtained from a lever that care should always be taken when using wrenches not to twist the bolt so that it breaks right off. Some modern wrenches fit into a hexagonal hole inside the nut or screw. Here the danger is to apply so much force that the hole is deformed into a cylindrical hole, after which no more twisting force can be applied.

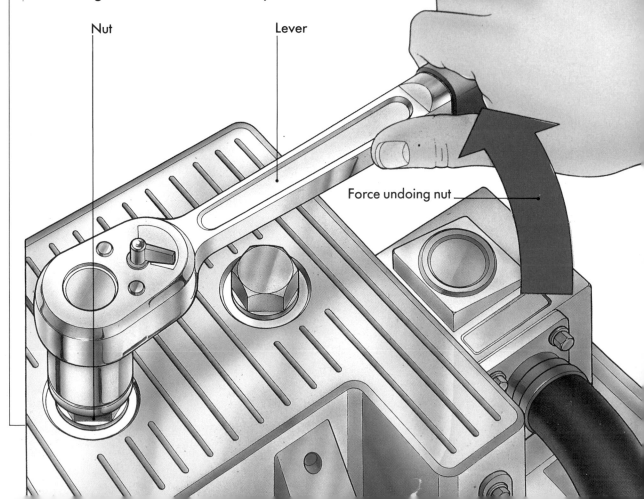

Nut

Lever

Force undoing nut

Gears and cogs are really a whole series of levers arranged around the outside of wheels. If the teeth on a pair of wheels are to match each other, the number of teeth will be proportional to the diameter of the wheel. So if the larger wheel is five times the diameter of the smaller one, it will have five times as many teeth. The small wheel will turn five times as fast as the big one, but the twisting force it can apply will be *reduced* by five times. Conversely, if twisting force is applied to turn the smaller wheel, five times the twisting force will appear in the larger wheel.

The shapes of gear teeth are cut so that as each new tooth in one wheel enters the space between two teeth in the other wheel, the surfaces of the teeth *roll* on each other rather than slide. As we saw earlier, rolling friction is a great deal less than sliding friction, and gear wheels should have as little friction as possible.

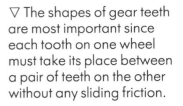

▽ The shapes of gear teeth are most important since each tooth on one wheel must take its place between a pair of teeth on the other without any sliding friction.

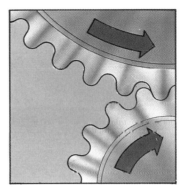

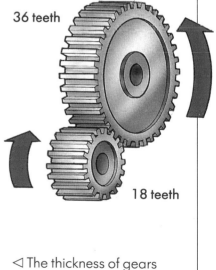

36 teeth

18 teeth

◁ The thickness of gears depends on just how much twisting force is needed. The gears must be thick enough to withstand the maximum twisting force without bending the teeth out of shape or breaking them off.

25

Inclined planes

An inclined plane is basically a slope, and slopes are often used to make work easier. It is much less difficult to push a load up a slope than to lift it straight up, because you appear to be working against a much smaller force of gravity.

When an inclined plane is bent around a central column, it becomes a screw. It has the same advantages as an ordinary inclined plane. A good example of the use of this is in a woodscrew. It can be driven into hard wood against considerable frictional forces.

Imagine an inclined plane made from a strip of cardboard bent to form a screw or spiral slide. If you cut a small strip from its outside edge to the central column, the strip would be the same shape as the blade of a helicopter. A wider strip cut in the shape of a rose petal would be the same shape as the blade of a screw that propels a ship.

The twisted inclined plane is a very powerful tool in the hands of the engineer. It is also one of the earliest pieces of engineering when used as the blade of a plow to turn over the top layer of soil in the earth. It enables large twisting forces to be applied continuously by means of a straight line force.

△ Pushing the wheelbarrow up the plank only needs about a quarter of the force that it would take to lift its contents *vertically*.

▷ An inclined plane, when twisted, produces a screw-like shape. This is the shape traced out by a helicopter blade as the machine rises into the air.

The rotating blades of a helicopter can even be seen as inclined planes for the air surrounding them. They force the air downward and thus receive a reaction force upward. This lifts the whole helicopter. In the same way the wings of an aircraft can be seen as straight inclined planes that deflect the air downward in order to get lift.

▽ The common woodscrew shows how the twisting force is converted into a very large straight vertical force. The taper on the screw helps it to force the wood apart to allow it to enter more easily.

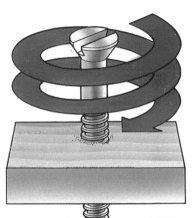

Expansion

Huge forces can be produced by heating objects or gases which then expand. This is the basis of all internal combustion engines. Fuel is injected into a cylinder containing a piston. The fuel is ignited and expands rapidly. This pushes the piston, which is then made to turn the wheels.

In some engines the fuel is ignited by an electric spark; in diesel engines it is ignited simply by the pressure produced by the returning piston. The instants when the fuel is injected, ignited and the waste products ejected all have to be carefully timed by mechanical linkages.

The explosions in the cylinder occur many times every second and a lot of heat is generated. Suitable cooling arrangements are a vital part of such engines.

▽ The piston is forced straight down by the pressure of the expanding gas. This motion is turned into rotation by a crank very similar to a bicycle pedal. It is made less jerky by having several pistons working on the same shaft which are fired at different times.

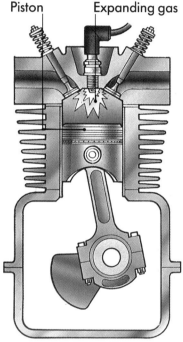

Piston   Expanding gas

◁ In small engines, such as those used for motorbikes, sufficient cooling of the cylinder is obtained by fitting fins to its outside. This increases the surface area from which heat can escape.

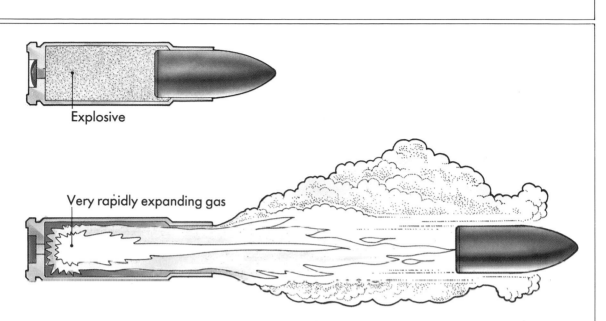

Explosive

Very rapidly expanding gas

Some of the biggest forces of all are produced in weapons designed to launch bullets and larger projectiles. Here explosive chemicals are turned from solid into gas with an enormous increase in volume. Again the explosion usually takes place in a cylinder, and the whole of the force is applied to the back of the missile, which is of relatively small area. The pressure on it is therefore very high. An equal and opposite force is applied to the launching device, causing it to kick back violently at the firing point. This is called the "recoil."

Chemical forces are not as efficient as they at first appear. Enormous force is applied as soon as the charge is fired. But as the gas expands, a lot of its energy is used in accelerating the gas itself.

Rocket propulsion goes one stage further. It uses the action and reaction principle that if you eject a mass of gas from one end of a tube, there will be an equal and opposite force on the tube itself. Rocket forces are therefore basically *inertia* forces. They are among the largest forces that humans have ever made.

△ When missiles are fired, they are often forced to travel in special grooves. This makes them spin as they are accelerated. The spin then keeps the missile flying in a straight line after it has left the tube.

29

Glossary

Acceleration

The rate of change of velocity with time, just as velocity is the rate of change of distance with time. Now distance has *direction* as well as length, so a change in *direction* means a change in velocity. In the same way a change of direction in velocity means that an acceleration is needed to produce it.

Speed is simply the distance gone in unit time and has *no direction*. Never confuse speed with velocity, even though their values may be, and generally will be, the same.

Engine

Any machine designed to produce mechanical work by converting it from some other source such as electrical (as in electric motors), chemical (as in gasoline engines, guns or rockets), moving water (turbine-driven power stations) or human effort (as in the bicycle).

Fluid

Anything that flows. It can therefore describe either a liquid or a gas.

Flywheel

A wheel whose main job is to use its inertia to reduce fluctuations in the rotational speed of a shaft. The best flywheels have the main bulk of their material concentrated in their rims.

Internal combustion engine

Name given to all engines which produce force by burning fuel *inside* a cylinder in order to push a piston. The force is produced by the expansion of the gas contained inside (usually air).

Lubrication

The process of reducing sliding friction between solids by introducing a layer of fluid between them. Fluid friction is less than sliding friction between solids. The most common lubricant is oil, although in modern technology air or other gas under pressure gives even better lubrication. Bearings built in this way are called "gas bearings," and whole surfaces covered with high pressure gas or liquid are known as "fluidized beds."

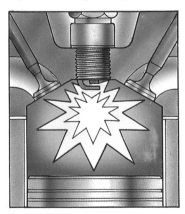

Expansion

Very large forces are generated by heating objects or gases in order to make them expand.

Friction

Friction forces always tend to oppose motion. They can be vitally useful or a great annoyance.

Gravity

The force of gravity pulls all objects toward the Earth and also, very slightly, toward each other.

Pressure

Pressure is the force exerted per unit area. Forces producing enormous pressures are often quite small. For example the force with which we close our jaws when we bite or eat food is not large. But the surfaces of our teeth which come in contact are so small that the pressure may rise to tons per square inch. It is pressure which breaks up the food rather than the size of the force.

Turbine

Name given to a special kind of engine in which rapidly moving fluid is deflected by blades mounted on a shaft. The blades are at an angle so that they act as inclined planes to the oncoming fluid. Deflection of the fluid in one direction by the blades produces reaction forces in the opposite direction on the blades, which then turn the shaft.

Viscosity

The frictional force in a fluid. It takes a force to propel a boat through water. It takes a force to pull a parachute down to Earth. In both cases the forces are generated by having to move the liquid or the gas (air). The friction occurs between particles of the fluid. Fluid friction is generally less than mechanical sliding friction, although some substances, like treacle, compete very well!

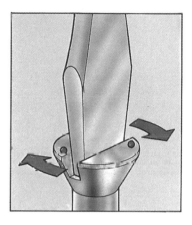

Parallel forces

When two parallel forces act in opposite directions on an object, they produce a *twisting* force.

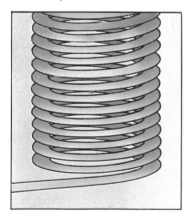

Inclined plane

The most useful form of inclined plane is bent around a central column in a spiral or helix.

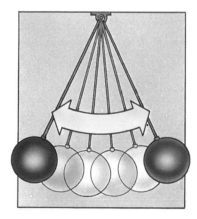

Inertia

Inertia tends to prevent objects from changing either their speed or their direction of motion.

Levers and gears

Levers and gears allow increase in the size of forces at the expense of longer movements.

31

Index